Resilience

Resilience

Emily Bilman

Resilience

Matador
9 Priory Business Park,
Wistow Road, Kibworth Beauchamp,
Leicestershire. LE8 0RX
Tel: (+44) 116 279 2299
Fax: (+44) 116 279 2277
Email: books@troubador.co.uk
Web: www.troubador.co.uk/matador

ISBN 978 1784623 159

British Library Cataloguing in Publication Data.
A catalogue record for this book is available from the British Library.

Printed and bound in the UK by TJ International, Padstow, Cornwall
Typeset in Aldine401 BT Roman by Troubador Publishing Ltd, Leicester, UK

Matador is an imprint of Troubador Publishing Ltd

For my parents

Contents

Acknowledgements

"The White Owl" was commended at the Stanza Competition and read out on National Poetry Day in October 2014 in London. Some of the poems in this collection were published in *Woolf*, Spring Issue 2015, Zurich, *The Headlight Anthology, Concordia University's Literary Journal, The Inspired Heart Anthology, Edition 3 & Inspired Heart Exclusive 4,* in Montréal, Canada; other poems were published in two *Iodine* issues, USA, in 5th issue of *Ygdrasil, Vol. XXII, Number 253, ISSN 1480-6401,* (May 2014), *Aois 21 Annual, San Diego Annual 2014-2015, Wilderness House Literary Review,* Boston, and *The London Magazine,* UK. "A River of Light" and an essay about Joost de Jonge are published in his book, *Painted Poetry & Painterly Poetics* which I edited. The book was published by The Authentic Art Agency, Utrecht, Holland, 2015. A few poems were read out at the American Mission in Geneva and broadcasted on World Radio Switzerland in Geneva in December 2014. Other poems were broadcasted on the BBC, UK. Two literary essays on T.S. Eliot's poetic personae have been published by the *The Journal of the T.S. Eliot Society,* UK.

RESILIENCE

RESILIENCE

Resilience

As I entered the tuff-earth's
Dark recesses, came in and out
Of her damp caves where I saw
Painted saints' clay-eyes, gashed
By envy-hands, I saw that Time
Hid and kept her garments
Ply upon ply, throughout Time.

The eater is, in turn, eaten in Time
Like a rodent-full reptile, claw-clutched
By an eagle, on its sovereign
Draft-steered sky-trajectory.

On my way to a new Byzantium
Of crystal, lace, amber, and gold,
I felt the freedom of my insight
Like a holy ethereal gift, Byzantium
Locked in Time's transient gyre,
Her icons, peacefully sifting
Their resilient inner seas,
Fixed with diamonds, pearls, sapphires,
Rubies within golden filigree-frames.

A River of Light

After Joost de Jonge's Archeology of Personhood, 3

A luminescent glass-cathedral,
Bright fuchsia, bright blue, bright purple,
Bright aquamarine where choir-voices
Celebrate a stained glass polyphony,
The river's primeval song, when
All was peace and light and beauty,
When the sun's colours begot Time,
When the first life was born with the warmth
Of primal movement, when the primal
Geometry of the first ochre curve and
The parallel elongation of the first form,
Bore the warm breasts of our brown world.

An Orange Sun

The trembling opalescent egg-yolk,
conveying heat to every cell
of my body, sustains my words,
maintaining sugar's metamorphosis

into light. The egg's membrane contains
the malleable, light-winnowing albumen
within its translucent net tying the sun-children

to the olympic games, their play-grounds,
pools, toboggans, tree-tops, swings,
space-hoppers, merry-go-rounds –

sun-sieved children playing hide-and-seek
with the sun beams seeping through the trees –
laughing, transfigured.

The Sky-Children

Sunlight streams in shafts metropolitan
Through the marbles of the portico.
In the harbour, subtle cargoes transport
The world's deep libido, Eros
Exposing, negotiating, buying, selling,
Transmuting goods for the well-being
Of the new sky-children.

In the agora, merchant voices
Are heard, negotiating among
The cloistered columns
Of the market, through light
And shade, the prices
Of oil, wine, and spice, the heft
Of gold, silver, copper, and lead
Discussing, in the market's shade,
The Aegean harbour's dues, speaking
Of the cold cargoes of
Cinnamon and cedarwood.

A sunlight surprise sieves through
The marbles of the merchant's
House where women gather to talk.
In the hall, glows a lion in mosaics, its mane
Burnished by tawny ochre shades.

The house's inner court transports the voices
Of the rose-maidens through its core –
Children playing with other children,
The mature aunt's plea
Reconciling the maiden with
Her mother-in-law who reproaches
Her with overspending, the elderly
Woman's voice speaking
To her grandchildren among
The serpentine court-marbles
Of chiaroscruro colours
Permeable to shadow
Permeable to light.

Halcyon Aura

Like the dove's innermost
bower-song, my voice's gradual
gestation grows into an intimate
voice held, hummed, hidden
in the hawthorn bower. Is it

the day's halcyon aura
that harmonizes the baby's
glossalalia with the dove's croon
in the hawthorn bower, the child asks.

The River

Sifting the river surreptitiously
until our gleaming eyes become
the sieve's Stygian eyes, until
our hands become the river's time,
we seek and sift the golden specks
to lighten our lives when the child
digs out the golden rule:
do not do to others what you
do not want others to do to you.
And he makes the river his own.

The White Owl

Clearing from the nocturnal fields
like the white owl, memory seized
us after we sang exile's bitter
herbs and drank the turbulent wine
that hurt us as your son, mourning
his mother's sudden death, rejected you,
tearing up the cheque you gave him.
You left. Like the impeccable
snow reflecting our inner peace, all
too suddenly, his striated eyes turned
inwards, a soaring whiteness,
barely spot-streaked, night-gliding

with wind-harnessed wings, crossed
our road, shearing our darkness.

The Morning Hawk

The hawk cleared out
of the tawny bog-field,
the world-womb, fogged
with steam-water and air,
and returned into the soil's
fullness, fretting its wide wings
against the grey watery sky,
vying its wide wings against
the huge chestnut like the metal
teeth of two gyres, scraping
against each other in the dense
water-air – then, the hawk flew
out into the morning light, swiftly
gliding from my eyes' memory.

The Traveller

"My love-life is a drag" you said.
I offered you my poetry's balm.

Like magnet-mirrors,
our eyes met in the night
as you related the story
of your parked car remaining
water-proof in the high tide
while you were partying.

I felt the bluntness of your car's metal
roof protecting your hurt heart from
the tide, your heart hurting silently
in its callous cage, waiting
for a wild wound to free you
as it once freed the hunter, Adonis.

A thousand wind-drawn doves
flying towards the sun
bond me with my memory,
my ecstasy of you. I feel
light, so light, so very light,
sun-playing with the star-edged
Aegean waves. My heart,
my veins, my lungs, my blood
pulsing, trembling, quivering
like Venus' wind-born anemone,
for your redemption on the prairie.

The Journey

Her mother wore a cream-colored head-
dress coiled around her forehead.
You cuddled, hugged and
kissed her blond baby-daughter,
holding her hands in yours,
yours. (A boy, we both wrongly thought.)

- "Her head-dress shrouds
her head as if she were a pilgrim
on her way to a purifying spring. Why
is her head swathed so?"

I asked, asked myself,
and then you. You moved closer.
"She is pregnant. Her head-dress
 hides her hairless head
 after chemotherapy."

We walked together on the cobble-
stoned old town under your umbrella
sheltering us, your umbrella
strolling, striding, pacing with us both,
our channel-words streaming
between two river-tides, racing
with the river's undertow, yet tied to us.

Like Sappho's visitor, lover,
you've come and gone and left me
darkling with questions.

The Inner Child

My melancholy dissipates
as I enter the hidden hermetic
forest that lifts its ethereal
chiaroscuro veil near
the water-source where
swans alight, aerating
their wings in the aegis
of the perennial waters.

Wide-eyed, in the clearing's
tamed light, I ask my inner child:
"how, will we, now and then,
in the lit clearing, meet?"

The Lady of Resilience

Like the multifoliate rose
softly unfolding within
her elongated hands,
The Lady of Resilience
holds her son's virtual intelligence
in her arms. My inner peace
grows as her eyes fix
the future of melancholy,
her silent sacrifice quietly
shaping my seas of desire
into the well-waters of fortitude.

THE STAIRWELL

The Stairwell

The empty space in the entrance hall
Is now ready to receive the winding marble
Structure that will lead to the bedrooms.
My brother and I have arrived
From our old terraced house by the sea
With our grandfather, the architect, to survey
The workers, excited at the installation,

The perfect fitting. But above the staircase,
We are seized by the round iron-cast mirror
That swallows our images like a huge surge-wave,
Distorting our faces with its ogre-hunger,

Transforming us into Goya's post-war paupers,
Lighting the war-broken streets with beacons,

To deliver expectant mothers from the blood-purge,
Save wailing infants from the unbroken dirge.

Vermeer's Love Letter

There's a sly complicity between the mistress
And her maid who gazes with pleasure
While the lady turns to her with an anxious
Anticipation as she holds the love-letter,
The palimpsest of her lover's passion.

He left her to sail on rich tumultuous shores.

Her painter-husband's camera obscura
Reproduces the scene from the slightly
Opened door of a dark side-room littered with
A creased map while she placidly reads
His letter in the comfort of her kitchen
Suffused with a white subdued light.

The framed painting, an intended indenture,
Feigns the fate of hand-to-hand adventure.

The Blood-Vessel

Like a virtual war-doll made
Of clay but bearing war-scars,
The soldier's broken legs were
Replaced by the surgeon-vessel
Of the oil-war, blood-framed for freedom.
No more fallen swamp-soldiers
Fighting ancient wars, death-bled
Like wild animals by stalking poachers.

His girl-friend bends upon the soldier's
Wheel-chair like the spectre of the thorn-shrub,
Arching its shadow on the begrimed
Land, lest it be scorched by burning oil.

My oil lamp's fading filigree-flame now lights up
The land's life and my green sentry-struggle.

Darkness Suspended

During a total solar eclipse

Birds frozen from their songs
                    dumbfounded –

dust-dilated black clouds fixed
by the dark-poised celestial magnet
on a stunned, synchronous sky
like an indigo tent-vault slowly
                cambering
          closing down down on me
until the new moon's shadow totally screens the sun
                chilling
the day's rain like dry spears
                 piercing the soil-shield.

Suddenly, darkness clears
as a sunbeam-couple elope
to swim in my eyes, bright
like the sparse silver specks
on the mollified kelt-skins
as the fish scent their way
through the current-cycles
to rejoice in the sun-sea

surviving their birth-river's
spawning, mourning mouth.

The Window

Outside the window there
is a straight street, its white
houses aligned up to the little
red house right opposite
my window; the street lights
are amber projectiles;
electric wires web the houses
and all of us each to each.

A Secret Language

For Lizzie

Like a suppressed melody set free
by a cello and a saxophone, we speak
in a language we invent on the spur
of the moment, improvising about
our complaints, too ancient to be recorded
in the valleys of Time, like the repressed
tongue of crime and punishment,
perhaps, reborn. She pours out her heart
to me with the cappriccio of her cello voice
about her punishments – an hour
without her Barbies, no access
to her Kitty kitchen, neither swings
nor the trampoline, only *bricolage*
for spending too much time on timeless
musings, walking away to search
for stray leaves in the streets,
collecting stones and pine-cones on the way
back from the kindergarten, dreams, dreams,
dreams streaming up like the saxophone's
breaths, blending her candid innocence
with my resonating alto-saxo voice.

Mother-of-Pearl Buttons

Starched like a dried-out potato,
the white cotton collar girdles
my neck uptight. The round
buttons of my black uniform
are mother-of-pearl eyes.
Suddenly, I hear my heart
beat as I recollect running,
running, running
with the other kids
quickly downhill
to touch the brick wall
with my wide-stretched
hands, shouting
first first and first.

Snapshots

The clicks feel sharp
Like a surgeon's scalpel
On the bare skin. Antiseptic
On the body beneath
My sleaveless green silk dress.

After the snapped photos, I feel
The sunlight seep silently through
The symmetrical plane trees planted
By my husband in the park leading
To the portico in front of our house.

The Rave-Parade

Made up like modern *tragediennes,*
Transvestite drag-queens dance
On rave-wagons. Acrobats, jesters,
Long-tailed felines, golden sculpted
Bodies, rainbow-tainted emperor
Butterflies in hot embrace,
A congregation of white-winged
Angels perform a motley love-dance.
The city's youth on fluorescent
Wheeled-wagons shake their
Heads in frantic techno beats.
Rockers, disguised as panthers,
Mime each other as they rave
On the longest chain-wagon
Slithering, sloughing, romping,
Through the heart of town – revelling.

EVERYMAN

Everyman

we are everyman
our eyes shine
like lamp posts
our words are
thwarted angels
each word, a gift
compensating guilt
we are Time's misfits
deceiving
each other
with fallen words
each word
a beguiling serpent
each word
mourning beauty
each word
love's martyr
we are everyman
our eyes shine
like light bulbs

The New Coming
a Yeatsian Paradox

Like felines stalking their prey
until death, we pursue
this fiery world with fleeing fury,
tenebrous, as if the distance
between the thieves
and the stolen goods

                    were virtual. The Oedipal riddle

still is riddle. Oedipus beckoning
blind – behind him, the city's locked
iron gates. Summoning. The sentinel-
sphinx, by cloud-shadows, oppressed.
Announcing. A blood-dolphin sea
of strife, mire, and crime. Double-dealings.
Everyman. The new man.

What stealthily frightening, shadowy,
leonine creature, subservient
like a feral virtual mask, pleading with me,
straggles towards Jerusalem to be born?
in the wilderness? at what wild price?

Holocaust

after Max Frisch's *Andorra*

By his name he is killed.

Shorn from himself, the boy
lies in the hands of the nazis.
His will broken, he now shuns
his heart's call, scorns his boss,
scorns his friends, scorns his surrogate
mother who stole to save him.

The villagers rage with prejudice.

Exorcised by the doctor, the mob's guilt
turns to public woe in neons of negation, while
in public indifference hands lie whitewashed.

Moving with the whiz of a whistle
Frisch's random robots form
a mute chorus as decreed
by the official yellow sheet.
In the main street of the village,
shoes lie allineated, waiting
for their rightful owners –

shoe after shoe only for the non-Jew.
Public fear is for everyone
only the idiot is spared.

Disowned twice by his shoes
the boy wills to die.
Despite the murder of a name by a name
somewhere in the world
a spare pair of shoes waits for him.

Though the world is burnt-out,
the self is death-transcendent

31

Hiroshima

the scorched city
imaplodes
through her core
in a nuclear cloud
irradiated
passers-by freeze
like silent suns
a fallen fog shrouds the river

Armageddon

Virtual warrior
burning
one of the three azaleas
(the one on the right)
on my window sill
triturating
all the blood-red flowers
stifling the day
you fought the fratricidal war

The New Warrior

masked warrior of the new century
immersed in new-born water
cleaning the debris of scraped ruins
among the dust and the rubble
breathing death-filaments into your lungs

                           the skeleton-ground
                           is moulting into new
                           synchronized worlds
                           locked beneath you

Cleanin' Asbestos

The sun is hot as a boiling magnet.
Behind our faceless mask-shields, we're safe!

– We're cleanin' asbestos between
 the walls, the racks, the scaffolds, the buildings.

 Like iron-filaments, asbestos
 germ-dust clings to our lungs,
 clogging our breath,
 constricting our lung-trees
 like dried-out sea-stars.

– Years after the duty-breach
 that led to the scandal, they paid
 us indemnity for insulating homes;
 but it's too late – like a cancer-sun,
 the asbestos-sun grew
 inside us . . . too late –
 the unquenchable guts
 in our throats rendered
 us voiceless with asbestos!

The tattoos on their sinewy arms, swollen
like liability bills, are the perennial rose-scars
bleeding inside their guts. No, behind their
faceless mask-shields, they were not safe!

The Sibyl

Wrapped in shawls and rags,
her hair, a myriad mess, the Sibyl
writhes in her yellow hut, whirling
her wheel into a crimson wrath.

The horsemen will steal the thunder torch.

The Sibyl's stealthy wheel conjures
Goya's paupers, elves, and harlequins.
The flying horsemen gallop across the river,
Cross the trenches, and enter the castle.

She should not linger in her thatched hut.

The Sibyl rocks her torso, implores the thunder.
With a final wrench, the horsemen wreck
the Sibyl's wriggling wheel of fortune.
They save the thunder torch.

Her hair's meshes are now sown seeds,
roses redeeming the horsemen's
gardens, war-torn with strife.

Bullying

Your skin's virtual memory feels
like the juvenile bull's sinewy skin,
smoldering under the sun – hot to my touch.
The two bulls were, then, beating the arena's sand
with their hooves. You, now, move closer and
touch my hand. One bull had darted head-on;
their horns had locked, pushing head-against-head,
until the loser left while the winner remained.
You, now, draw closer to kiss me. I recoil.
Like the darting bull, you insist –
insist. My heart speeds. Wide-eyed,
I watch you as I watched the bulls
while your breath freezes my mouth
and you embrace me like
the winner bull that bolted
towards me, burning horns first –
then, was elbowed by his tender out
of the arena under the rutting crimson sun.

The Hunter

The kestrel-eyed hunter stalks
The stag through the forest
And shoots it.
Through the heart,
The stag falls.

He flays the hide from
The skin, cuts the flesh up,
Slicing its blood-stained
Thick fuming layers
Into large hunks.

The children ogle
The barbecue-coals
Sparkling like the hunter's
Fiery kestrel-eyes.

Fledglings

I watch the yellow and crimson-
streaked kestrel, meticulously
spear-gutting, string by lithe string,
the morning song-thrush, claw-clutched,
death-stiffened on my garden-grass.

In my own nest
the piles and piles
of tablets and pills veined
like tawny open fox-
gloves in a stub field,

the stacks of paper-clips
and staples like barley-
sheaths smoothing, stirring,
waking the wind

the pencils and pens, perennial
like the velvet-stalked immortelles,
the mounds of cardigans, shirts,
sweaters and scarves,
shedding their colours
like pomegranates broken
on the maquis in the late fall:
these I sort out and recycle
and vertiginously, circum-
scribe them into grey debris bags.

Stunned

Like the robin in its first flight,
Her heart flew out from her rib-cage.

With her lethargic body, sluggish
Like a wrinkled parchment,
He leads her up the goat-trail
Upon the hill, stone-cast with
Juniper, wild thyme, and briar.

Her hollowed head infused with
The valley's effluvium,
They climb higher and higher,
Lying down among the thistle
And the thorns at sun-set.

The sun-rays irradiate upon
His iron axe as he hits her to keep
His blood-pledge with the sun-god,
To warrant his corn-covenant
With the weary barren land.

The Hunt

He aligned the ruffed grouses
On a string and tied them each
To each. His lithe hands kindled
The barbecue. I dug deep into
The gored crimson of their hearts,
Bitter offerings to the sun,
Firm with fire-filaments.

The Sauna's Shadow

The city's war-maimed marble
monuments lie desecrated. Roaming
among the urban scaffoldings
concealing blood-fields, I enter a sauna.
Will the heat cleanse me
and the war-ridden city?

Inside the stifling shadow
of the ophite sauna, I disclose
my tatooed serpent.

> As the serpent slithers
> down my backbone,
> fault-filaments
> clog my skin-pores
> like mercury drops.
>
> In his stubborn denial,
> a tenebrous man lowers
> his head, rejecting temptation.

Simple Toys

Sunlight sifts through the fortified
Walls of the crusader-city by the sea,
Trodden by merchants and warriors,
Where I was a child-carer
Inventing games, cooling
Their ill fever with lullabies while
In the city, the predator roamed.

Mixed with the scent of sea-brine,
The force of the new-wine that we tasted at lunch
Now flows into my chronicle-memory.

A boy clacking his wagon against
The cobblestones is watching us
Holding hands on the bench.

Facing the sea's freshness, the boy
Turns away as we kiss.

You say children are satisfied with simple toys.

Fallen Symmetry

I thought I saw a youth
lying by the water-reeds
on the banks of the mother-river
stretching his long legs
under the shadowy moonlight,
supine after a day's fishing
by the river fertile with pike
and the giant carp.

No, he lay there by the reeds,
ambushed, by the mother-river's
banks, fetus-folded, dust-broken,
his figure immersed in Dürer's
glaucous livid light like Christ
stretched in pierced symmetry.

The New Everyman

He is the antihero
Of our alterity.
A man meeting
The man trying
To make sense
Of it all, laughing,
Making us laugh.
Feeling his own skin
After a virtual death
He looks for home.
He is born again.
Still looking for home,
He faces death
And asks us never
Ever to look back.
And he dies.

THE TEMPEST

THE TEMPEST

The Tempest

Swathed in cellophane, the beryl-beach
Breathes out a mineral translucence.
The wild western wind swells the dunes
With brine, waves are born within
Surge-waves whose crests foam
Like horses' mouths. The wind dwindles
The jade-sea into a tidal pool. Swaddled
By rival currents, I am born between
Two waves. Like a twirling laser torch,
The jade-light tears the flying foam,
Shears the brine, sprays the pungent
Air with ions of iodine. A salt-statue

Gripped by the electrifying light,
I am hypnotised by the sea's plight.

Water on My Skin

Like orchid-wombs bursting
to sunlight in their primal impulse,
my skin-pores open up to warm water,
each warm jet, loosening my vertebrae
into free-floating chains. Water, the purifier,
cleans my body; like the sea-spray,
fresh water gleans my skin-pores,
quenches my thirst, refreshes me.

Once saved from tidal waters swollen
like a woman's womb, you,
for whom I, no longer, thirst,
courted me, bent on your knees
like a valorous knight. Elated,
I soared above the city-roofs.

A Madrigal

Your face, my love, flows
Into the river's voice,
Sweeping grains of gold
From the grit-rocks towards
The mountain tamed by us.

Our two faces touch
Under the icy moon-gleam
That disentangles the silvery
Silhouette of the oak,
Our large framed shelter.

A madrigal at dawn leads
Your hands on my breasts
In our silk-smooth satin bed
Soft like the summer's river-bed.

Hyperion

Hyperion bore the sun in his bosom,
The crimson fire-ball of life that warms us,
Bore the moon and the tides that sculpt our shores,
Saving the dawn form the deluge, falling in
And out of love with the seasons and the sun.

Like us. Clasped in a love-knot with each other,
Our souls heat up like Hyperion's sun-core,
Warming us as they whirl. Passionate, yet
Insubstantial, the firmer our cores, the stronger
Our love grows as we flow into each other's mould
Like those distant revolving binary stars
Feeding on each other's fuel. And in this world

Of brief nymphs, we sustain our romance
With our love's perpetual sustenance.

Love's Palimpsest

Photogenic with anxious anticipation,
Vermeer's lady holds her lover's letter,
his passion's palimpsest,
in her oceanic hand while with the other
she holds her cithare. I imagine her
reading the letter as he chose her
for the fulfilment of his nuptial desire
despite the distance separating them.

I imagine his relief when he wrote
to her of his need for freedom
that he could now enjoy only with her.
I imagine the random excitement
that lit up her troubled eyes with
the reciprocal light of bonding and blood.

The Estuary

A water where
the ebb-wave, flood-born
is flood-broken yet
the wave wavers and transports
me through the river's dam

into the ocean. A flood-broken
ebb-wave where the slime sucked
below the swell, oozes
the surface light through
its dun density,
an ochre silt mass lulled by
the wave's gliding gait.

A water whose slime
slides under the wave's swelling skin
whose slime settles through the light's
silence winnowing through a prism

and between the ebb and the flux
billow-buoyed mud
suffuses
my melancholy
with the fluid mnemonic snapshot
of the estuary

where the mud flood faints
waywardly weaning
new fluent transfers
in sleek serpentine streaks
of deep oceanic blue.

L
   I
      M
        B
          O

like sinewy cats
slithering through
the nocturnal bushes
we bend our bodies stealthily
as the Limbo bar
is lowered further
for the next Limbo.
We're two maidens
bearing our poised water-jugs
high on our heads.
You are a fleur-de-lys,
in a white lace Creole
dress and I, an exotic
silk orchid, our syncopated
bodies bending under the

      L
        I
          M
            B
              O

Unquenchable

On the ocean's mobile weft, the wind
Stirs my vision with the speed
Of new-born cells. Palliative.
I breathe in the iodine, taste
The sea-brine and feel satiated.

Time raises the tides.

With the surge, seas pour into
Seas but these waters are still
Not enough to drown our thirst.
Inside dried-out wells, thirst boosts
Our craving with buckets of greed.
We dig another well and gather
Around it for water. Unquenchable.

Doves on Horses

I hear cello notes
The tears of a summer sea
Doves sing on horses

Light in my sea-suit,
Like an aquamarine skin,
I dive into the ocean

I dive for coral
Gulls dive for silver-finned fish
Doves move on horses

The Ocean

The ocean swells with vital currents.
Silver-skinned waves stir my imagination.
Dolphins dance and swerve with the waves.

Mottled pestrels fly out with excitement.
I daydream with the dolphin-songs.
The ocean swells with vital currents.

An albatross shrieks across the sky.
Anglers slide; shrimps slither into deep caves.
Dolphins dance and swerve with the waves.

Eels writhe their lithe bodies like serpents,
Chasing shrimps in the chirascuro sea.
The ocean swells with vital currents.

Whales sing, whales whisper, whales cry.
Sea-bass swim above the dark abyss.
Dolphins dance and swerve with the waves.

Plankton glimmer in the ocean-warp.
Waves weave my daydreams into a poem.
The ocean swells with vital currents.
Dolphins dance and swerve with the waves.

Silver Sails

Carve your sails in silver
And watch the wind clear
The cloud-strewn sky
For the sailboats.
Let the yellow-beaked
Albatross draw on the cerulean sky
Silver lines
Filled with words.

Shape
/ \
link   adjust

Every silver-word
Each to each
Like silver charms

    f
   a
  s
   t
    e
     n
     e
     d

On every verse.

THE CONTROVERSY

The Controversy

Daylight seeps on the book of hours
Inside his room, the world's microcosm.

Hidden from the world-spirit that brightened
The colours of the countryside, he reflected
On the futile alchemy of salvation during the plague,
His despair on dry parchment.

Was there no escape from thought? The dog
Ran around the room unleashed.

Did the *Word* precede the *Deed?* And can the *Deed*
Save our *Action* on the world? *Being* kept him safe –
Action was necessary.

If the *Word* preceded everything, why did he lack
The right words, time after time? Words lived in the shadow
Of words, fleeing their meaning. Doubt tore his tattered faith.

Soaring above the roofs of the world, he recollected *la piéta.*

Could the valor his lost love, her candor, merely be
His projection of the whole world's goodness on her figure?

The dog gnawed at his door.
His scavenger-foil stalked him like a hyenna.

Facing his foil, he felt weak like a sheathless
Poplar in the underworld, trapped
In the room of his remorse,
Between *the* pact and the world.

Soaring above the roofs of the world, he recollected *la piéta.*

Tempted by the virtual omnipotence
Staked against his soul by his foil,
He expiated at the stake of his guilt
At the smouldering stake of his beloved.

The Epidemic

Plague germs steal in with the sunset
through the shores into the arteries of the city,
through the round, hairy, curved, bony backs,
by the spry tails of the panic-stricken rats.

Sisyphus, the plague's harbinger,
stifles his scapegoats' gasps
under heaps of stone where
he hides the havoc of his loot.

In the playhouse, one body of rumour,
the rows behind me babble, babble, babble
like crickets creaking above a cloud of crops,
busy-bodying in trifles, interrupting each other,
imprisoning the actor within their power-antennae.

Like the maddened mob ripping,
then throwing the ugly features of their faces
upon their scapegoat to mock, then slay him,
the audience sunders the actor from his stage.

A lost automaton,
Sisyphus rolls to the hill's top
the ceaseless rock of his ill-spent guilt.

In the city, the plagued choir-child yells out his accursed,
yet cleansed guts to the white deafness of a bed-ridden ward.
Despite Sisyphus' ghost hovering over the urban plague,
the healer, my bondsman, gleans the boy's final scream
like a tiller burrowing, ploughing, planting his soil's plot.

A Hostage

Trapped in dead-ends hard to escape,
Helpless like a snared animal stripped

Of its fur for greed, torn from all ties, I am
Enslaved by the predator's double-tongue.

My love is shattered with rapacious lies
Until emptiness trounces my despair.

Beguiled by the tempter's tricks, I am
Imprisoned within a maze of fear.

I am like a tree ripped from its roots, rotting
In the soil of discontent. Like Faust,

My soul's integrity is staked against
A false future that constantly eludes me.

Remorse

Is a fallen kernel that pierces the throat,
Guilt that paralyses the hand for plucking
The flower before it blooms in the sun.

Guilt is the child of chaos, darkening
The room-sheltered mind, vexing thought,
Biting the heart like a sharp-toothed beast.

Remorse chooses the worm-infected apple
Instead of the immaculate fruit's innocence,
Yielding to temptation, choosing to abide

By the Fall even if the Fall leads to another's
Remorse and the belated awareness that the other's
Fate might, against all odds, out-fate our own.

Blindness

Like two coal-rods, your orphan-eyes lock
Out my heart's light with their hidden fire.

Like carnivorous plants closing in
On the translucent insect's green

Shield, your eye-masks hide you
From temptation, restraining our love's

Flow, impeding my inspiration. Yet,
Our oasis ripens with palm-dates and

The river-words flow from your mouth
As, with jokes and laughter, you strew

Golden grains of humour and fun
On all of us yet imprison my lost

Tears in your obsidian-eyes and
Our words within these sonnet-walls.

Dusk at Elm-Hill

Like a time-warp, the coiled
winding street draws me in
as I face the latticed windows
of the Strangers' Club, my dusk-vision
torn by time-breaches. The red brick
merchant house leans towards me
as I wander into a familiar inner
court that once was our sun-lit atrium.

I, now, stand dreaming by the goods-wharf,
the Wensum, like a subterranean
rumour, gleaning my mourning
willows, gathering my script-words.

The burnt beams of the weaving
room close in on me as I am coerced
to confess the wool-merchant's
ruin, the death of his plagued sheep –
faults I feigned. Led to the elm-stave
by the river – I, the maybe-witch,
my strength shorn, suffocate
at the stake of your seared light.

The token of a wicker witch
you so fearfully disowned, now burns
as, once, credulous in our future,
you reached out for my hurt hand
shorn from yours.

Cloned

hybrid-mammals, half-cobra, half
chameleon-like demons split
the earth that nurtures the sage, myrtle,
and the mint, the branches that sustain
the vintage vine.

half-goat, half-sheep shoats invade the farms.
skins of slain serpents are incrusted
on the bee-hives. sprayed with specific.
brewed in glass alembics.
breathless bees suffocate.

we conjure the clones for our defense.

their tongues curved as scythes,
"trespassers must die!" cry the cows
"for driving us mad with the food
meant to foster us."

Ghosts

With their handless hands,
ghosts trickle down the trapped
water-holes between the walls,
dripping down with water. Spidered
walls creak as they slide from
earthly spheres into wider spheres.
Ghosts hide behind closets,
become warped clocks covered
with mildew-webs invading warm
rooms, rotting the plants.
Dust-gloved ghosts collide
with unknown human hosts,
dispersing Time's dust.

Daemons

Like plebeians cracking the concrete,
sieve-mixing the urban silt-sands,
drill-digging the city's womb,
scooping and smiting the streets
with jackhammers to cable the city,

my-daemons-in-chaos vie with my synapses
for ideas linked to metaphors as an old poem
is made into a new one and I circumscribe
new symbols on words – re-read and
re-write, roused by an unrequited love –

played by Orpheus' lamenting
lyre, recalling Eurydice dying.

Eros, An Allegory

after Bronzino's "Allegory with Venus & Cupid" ~1545

Deceit, your hands are the tools of impunity.
You hold a honey-comb inside one palm,
A bitter scorpion-sting inside the other.
Pleasure, your child-prisoner, laughs as he scatters
Roses to Venus and Cupid in their nuptials.

Sly as a straying vixen, Deceit, you stare
Fraudulently at the erotic love scene
From your niche: your white body is born
From serpent-scales while your face of
Marble-melancholy is broken by reproaches.

A satyr and a masked nymph lie at Venus's feet.
Old man Time and the livid female mask of Oblivion
Compete for this regal gift behind a blue silk drapery.
Pleasure and Deceit, sculpted from soft marble-flesh,
Vie, throughout, to bait and abet lust against Love.

The Trench Coat

Tough-to-the-touch in my mother's
Trench coat and black crochet-gloves,
Keepsakes that I took from her post-mortem
Room, I trod the trail near the water-
Ways, trench-broken for turf.

Moon-struck, as I strode
The tenebrous trail, there appeared
Calliope, raising the tides. Like Abigail,
Fighting the hypocrites in *The Crucible,*

Prompting Miller's fall, I began
Crying, the next morning, in my carell
For missing my meeting with
The playwright twice – after
My mother's fatal fall and before
His death when I liberated my lease,
And with my fasting son, fixed
The broken T.V. at home –

In-breathing the acrid breath
Of his day's duty, pleading the release
Of his unreedeemed greed.

Renunciation

Like ageing Frost, solitary,
broken and blind, consigning
his despair to the frozen moon
as he renounced to his light, in saccades,
but kept up his dialogue with the icy night,
a quiet light to no other but ourselves,
we renounce meat, sugar and salt,
chocolate and alcohol, almost

virtually. Disembodied, our solitudes lie
besieged by the tenebrous winter moon,
as we rename the silence of our homes.

Others gather their long-expected fruits
yet I, after nurturing those fruits through
the seasons, still wait and wait, solitary.

TRANSFIGURATION

Apocalypse

A dark deep wound seeping inside me
like mud-in-water, settling as you take off
for more comfort for your wounded leg –
A dark deep foreboding omen, the severing of kith
from kin, the severing of children from their mother,
your victim-hands dissevered from your gangrened
arms – the eater, in time, eaten, ambushed,
as in the Trojan holocaust — the Trojan usurping,
the Greek, raping, kidnapping, molesting
to possess the other's carnage – sacrificial limbs
consumed – Agamemnon against Memnon –
Nestor dragged through his brother's dust –
young stabs, young sores incorporated
for more land, more horses – your food, your women,
your names made my own – a bone-heap burning
daily – my pyre-dirge, your Trojan vigil-urn.

My dark deep wound of doom,
seven serpents springing from my waist,
my maiden-metamorphosis into the sea-monster
Scylla, my hands gripping the spawning eel,
the slimed devil-fish – your myriad fright-dogs
barking inside me. My dark deep wound
warning me against the moving mud where you,
as a maiden, fell, oozing your child-like candor
like the Charybdis whirl-pool swallowing
my six seamen, my throbbing bronchi,
my breathing sinews into a mud-turmoil settling
inside me one Saturday afternoon, foreboding,
shearing me from my petals as a poppy
in the wind, bereaved, as towards Hades,
you who always stood by me, took off
in an aura of fatal light.

In-Voiced by Time

My back, in custody, is usurped
By Achilles' ire. A thousand

Soldiers drain the Trojan
Horse of the holocaust.

In iridescent rings of fire, the pain
Radiates down my spinal-kiln

While my ill-spent rage is sealed
Within a golden filigree pill-box.

Like a Spartan, I swallow the pain-killer
To cool down my body's chthonic coals.

Time's Turmoil

Peeping in with the mover
through the cellar door into suitcases
bloated like sturgeons' silver-dotted
bellies bulging, bursting, breaking
with roe-swarms, ready for removal.

Suddenly, the utter panic
of lost keys, and I, locked out
of the flat where you had fallen down –
your ruptured time, shattered
into specks of light until the morphine
shot on your leg brought you,
in emergency, out of yourself
into *my* river of light.

Bills, complaints, invoices, letters-of-the-law,
labeled and stamped,
an introvert, queued I
in panic, I lingered in lethargy
on a late afternoon at the law-
yer's lounge
listing witnesses
for the defense of my lease;

then, packed, packed – packed china
plates with green fruits and leaves-in-relief
between soft tissue sheets for the charity
in the suburban warehouse; packed
wine, whisky, water glasses upon glasses;
packed away the dress you wore for my wedding,
hand-painted ferns and lilac lilies on black
silk muslin; packed up my time-in-mutiny,
a river rushing backwards

to its source-wrath on its tragic trajectory
for a new flat negotiated with a double warranty.

The New Millennium

In memoriam of my mother

I found you lying on the parquet floor, jouncing
your head to and fro, convulsing, weeping
to unlock the prison of your remorse.
I descended to the wine-cellar to obtain
an estimate for my move while you slipped
on the mongrel carpet. In pain, you wept
to cleanse your guilt of falling - perhaps,
wept to cleanse the guilt of destroying
your aging leg-prothesis or seeing me
off after providing me with a warranty
for my new flat. Or, maybe, you wept
for a conflicting mixed motive,
unknown to me, repressed by you,
on account of my brother. You said
you felt two ghost-hands on your back,
pushing you down. And, with your force,
you clutched the antique butter-press oak
lamp like a life-buoy – a rustic butter-press
I had transformed into a lamp for the cozy
living room, decorating its long cone-shade
with a rugged beige wild-silk fabric. Utterly pale,
you wept without tears as I stroked
your temples with both of my hands until
the ambulance steered you towards Lethe.

Father

The sweat on the wrinkled skin
of the autumn apples, the scent
of ochre-crimson apple-pulp fermenting
in the fireplace, remind me of my father,
a standing skeptic on our summer balcony,
his arms, nude, his sun-lit body, facing
the bronze statue of the physician, his mentor,
in the teeming city whose residents
he diagnosed with precision and
cured with compassion, at times,
accepting eggs, oil, or honey for his fees.

Amazed

Amazed as Daedalus in the humid
density of the early city, I entered
the shopping mall, an urban
labyrinth-in-motion. I crossed
Picasso's acoustic thinkers, suspended
in Time with their iron kettles and
tin guitars, as they wedged into Time's wheel,
scraping stridently against Time's teeth.
Like a puppet fastened by the length
of the six or seven-eyelet strings I bought
for my shoes, I was too blind to see
that the urban dampness welling up in me
would shape my Minotaur-self into a winged
sonnet as I soared above the city's seamless sea.

Breakthrough

Like the glass-maker's lit breath
entering the red hot molten glass-belly
as he blends liquid colour
into the glass core, swirling

the fire-plasma into shape, I break
into language with light
traversing each word, with light
on everything, on every word

transmuting every poem,
transporting the crowds, the oceans
like lit water-swathes scattering, and
unscathed, gathering myriad crystal specks

bathing beast, bird, bug,
man and woman in light, alike.

Time

Like wave into wave, Time
pours into time's daily frame
as I daydream – gliding, breathing,
soaring above the cloud-swarms
like a swan. Within the shadows
of Hades, Time, that highway
speeding to its source, recedes
within my sealed eyes where
empyrean skies unfurl.

Circles

acts of time are synchronous
with Time suspended
in cosmic action
like the harmony of circles
within concentric circles
swan mirroring swan
in circular courtship
Time redeeming
time present

The Arc

A magnet-in-motion or a mobile eye
A galactic lens possessing perception-at-will,
The virtual bequeather of virtual lore
Arches its way into my primal sight.

The Pronk

the grass
juts fresh
with rain
bodies bend
by grace
juvenile
gazelles
jump
with joy
leap up
spread
musk
in the air
predators
flee

Mimesis

The man by the rocks disposes
The red plastic sheets littering
The thick white rope that ties
The boat to the lacustrine port.

He turns to his wife for approval.

The female swan cleans the waters
From the thick weeds by the rock's mouth
Shuffling the waters to free nutrients
For her brood that gently swills.

I watch the swan and the man miming each other.

The brown-grey juveniles glide
Between the two white summer swans
Under the bridge on the crystal lake.

Couples should mime swans, the poet says.

The
Three
Arches

As I walk, I see three
successive arches
leading each
to each, opening into
inner courts, fountains,
gardens in the sun,
a round, sudden
fire-ball, sun-rays
winnowing through the arcs,
forming arch-shadows
within Time.

The Creed-City

Masons, in my creed-city, carve
Peace out of stone, polishing
Obsidian into myriad mirrors.

Masons, in my creed-city, glaze
Colour into myriad mosaics,
Shaping a virtual bestiary.

In my creed-city, I ferment
Rye-beer and barley-bread
And offer bread to the masons.

Illuminated

"David Composing his Psalms", a painting
in *The Byzantine Paris Psalter* (867 AD)

like a manuscript
the anointed child-king
personifies the goats
in his psalms with their horns
jutting out
of the illuminated page
as his three-faced muse holds
with pastoral melancholy
the child-king's laurel
scroll within
parched ochre frames

like my toil's source
mosaic-waters

The Corn Cradle

Steered by the swallows, tents
are planted on the land, the cradle
of corn, olive, sage, fig and barley.
In the wild thorn and thistle fields,
I tend the goats, as they bolt
against the shrubs, ejecting stones
as they slip downhill, an indigo cloak
screening my skin from the arid swirling

dust. Along sombre shades of path,
darkness slowly descends upon
the sand-fields. A yellow-eyed leopard
stalks the night, abruptly leaping
into the artery of its nuptial prey.
The star-designed sky-roof shields us.

Transfiguration

The woman singing with her desert-voice
transformed the sky and the sand,
the nomad sitting by the barren bush
into one seamless immensity. The mirage
changed into the spring-water, streaming
along the orange groves in the oasis,
between the palm and date trees
by the well yet the transient mirage
of her face, gazing through the round
wheel-window, could not be effaced.
Her mirage-face still trembles
in my imagination while the sun blazes
on the scintillating sand-dunes
and the desert's redeemed bushes.

Author's Biography

EMILY BILMAN writes poetry and literary criticism in Geneva where she represents London's Poetry Society and hosts poetry meetings. She earned her Master of Fine Arts in Writing from Vermont College, and her PhD from East Anglia University where she taught literature. Her poetry book in French is entitled *La rivière de soi.* An amateur astronomer, she is a member of Les Poètes de la Cité and the Geneva Writers Group. She is a regular contributor to literary magazines in the Humanities. She has given poetry readings in Geneva, France, Spain, England and USA and read her poems on the BBC and on World Radio, Geneva. Her doctoral thesis entitled, *The Psychodynamics of Poetry: Poetic Virtuality and Oedipal Sublimation in the Poetry of T.S. Eliot and Paul Valéry,* demonstrates her theory of literary creativity, named "virtuality". *Modern Ekphrasis,* a book on the philosophy of art, and on the painting-poetry analogy, was published in 2013. She is a poetry editor. Emily's most recent poetry books are entitled *A Woman By A Well* and *Resilience.*

http://www.emiliebilman,wix.com/emily-bilman
ch.linkedin.com/pub/emily-bilman/13/664/376/en

Publications

Breakthrough in *The Psychodynamics of Poetry*, LAP, Saarbrücken, 2010.

Resilience, Breakthrough, Attar of Rose, Cleanin' Asbestos
in *The Inspired Heart, Edition 3*, Melinda Cochrane International, Montréal, Canada, 2013.

The Journey, The Traveller, The Morning Hawk, Apocalypse, The Ocean, Renunciation
in Ygdrasil, Vol. XXII, Issue 5, Number 253, May 2014. ISSN 1480-6401.
http://users.synapse.net/kgerken

Eros, Bullying, The New Millenium
in *The Inspired Heart Exclusive 4*, Melinda Cochrane International, Montréal, Canada, 2014.

Halcyon Aura, The Window, The Sky-Children, The Child in *Iodine Poetry Journal*, Vol. XV, No. 2, Fall/Winter 2014/2015.

Vermeer's Love Letter, Water On My Skin, The Tempest
in *Aois21 Annual*, September 2014, VA USA.

The Estuary
In *The London Magazine,* June-July issue, 2014.

The White Owl was a commended sonnet
in the Stanza Poetry Competition in London on September 23, 2014.

Dusk at Elm Hill
in *The San Diego 2014-2015 Annual*, USA.

Everyman, The New Everyman in *Iodine Poetry Journal*, Vol. XVI, No. 1, Spring/Summer 2015

An Orange Sun, Amazed, Transfiguration in the on-line issue of Wilderness House Literary Review #10/1, Boston, Spring 2015. http://www.whlreview.com

Fledglings in Headlight Anthology 18 – *Lacunea*, Concordia University's Literary Magazine, Québec, Canada, 2015.

The Corn-Cradle, Space, A River of Light in *Woolf,* Spring issue, Zurich, 2015.